SCHOLASTIC

Informational Passages
for Text Marking & Close Reading

GRADE 3

By Marcia Miller & Martin Lee

NEW YORK • TORONTO • LONDON • AUCKLAND • SYDNEY
MEXICO CITY • NEW DELHI • HONG KONG • BUENOS AIRES

Teaching *Resources*

Cover design: Brian LaRossa
Interior design: Kathy Massaro

Photos ©: 14: Courtesy of Ed Ritenour/The Lamplighter School; 16: Royal Photographic Society/NMEM/Science & Society Picture Library; 18: Courtesy of The Franklin Institute; 20: David R. Frazier/Photolibrary, Inc./Alamy Images; 22: cscredon/iStockphoto; 24: Aivolie/Shutterstock, Inc.; 26: Romaoslo/iStockphoto; 28 top: aarrows/Shutterstock, Inc.; 28 bottom: Wolgin/Shutterstock, Inc.; 30: boggy22/iStockphoto; 32: Aristide Economopoulos/The Star-Ledger/The Image Works; 34 top: Ethan Kan/Flickr; 34 bottom: jejim/Shutterstock, Inc.; 36: Do van Dijk, NiS/Minden Pictures; 38: PeopleImages/iStockphoto; 40: Levi Strauss & Co. Archives; 42: janeff/iStockphoto; 44: Selfiy/Shutterstock, Inc.; 46: Jessica McGowan, Atlanta Journal-Constitution/AP Images; 48: monticello/Shutterstock, Inc.; 50: Aleksandr Sulga/Shutterstock, Inc.; 52: Christopher Futcher/iStockphoto.

ISBN: 978-0-545-79379-7
Copyright © 2015 by Scholastic Inc.
All rights reserved.
Printed in the U.S.A.
Published by Scholastic Inc.

4 5 6 7 8 9 10   40   22 21 20 19 18 17 16

Contents

Informational Text Passages

Main Idea & Details

Sequence of Events

Fact & Opinion

Compare & Contrast

Cause & Effect

Context Clues

Problem & Solution

Summarize

Make Inferences

Author's Purpose

Introduction

The vast majority of what adults read—in books, magazines, or online—is nonfiction. We read news stories, memoirs, science pieces, sports articles, business e-mails and memos, editorials, arts reviews, health documents, assembly or installation instructions, advertisements, and catalogs. Informational reading, with its diverse structures, formats, and content-specific vocabulary, can be demanding.

Many students enjoy reading nonfiction, but navigating the wide variety of rich informational texts poses challenges for evolving readers. Students may lack sufficient background knowledge of a topic or be unfamiliar with specific vocabulary related to it. In addition, they may find some structures or features of nonfiction puzzling. This is why exposing students more frequently to complex informational texts and introducing them to active reading-comprehension strategies are now key components of successful reading instruction. Useful strategies, clearly taught, can empower readers to approach informational texts purposefully, closely, and independently. Such active tools provide students with a foundation for success not only in school, but for the rest of their lives.

> **Connections to the Standards**
>
> The chart on page 9 details how the lessons in this book will help your students meet the more rigorous demands of today's reading standards for informational text.

Text Marking: A Powerful Active-Reading Strategy

To improve their comprehension of complex informational texts, students must actively engage with the text. Careful and consistent text marking by hand is one valuable way to accomplish that. To begin with, by numbering paragraphs, students can readily identify the location of pertinent information when discussing a piece. By circling main ideas, underlining supporting details (such as definitions, descriptions, evidence, explanations, and data), and boxing key vocabulary, students interact directly with the material, making it more digestible in the process. But the true goal of teaching text marking is to help students internalize an effective close-reading strategy, not to have them show how many marks they can make on a page.

Purposeful text marking intensifies a reader's focus. It helps readers identify information as they read and recognize and isolate key details or connect relevant ideas presented in the text. For instance, boxing words like *before, next, finally,* and *after* can clarify the sequence of ideas or events in a passage. By circling expressions like *I think* or *in my opinion,* students learn to discern opinions from facts. When students are asked to compare and contrast information in a passage, boxing signal words and phrases, such as *both, in the same way,* or *however,* can make identifying similarities and differences more apparent. Words like *since, because of, due to,* or *as a result* signal cause-and-effect relationships that structure a piece. Furthermore, the physical act of writing by hand, in itself, helps students not only process what they read, but remember it as well.

The 20 reproducible passages in this book, which vary in genres and forms, organizational structures, purposes, tones, and tasks, address ten key reading-comprehension skills, from identifying main ideas and details, and separating facts from opinions to summarizing and making inferences. Consult the table of contents to see the scope of skills, genres, forms, content areas, and Lexile scores of the passages. The Lexile scores fall within the ranges recommended for third graders. (The scores for grade 3, revised to reflect the more rigorous demands of today's higher standards, range from 520 to 840.)

Each passage appears on its own page, beginning with the title, the genre or form of the passage, and the main comprehension skill the passage addresses. The passages include visual elements, such as photographs and illustrations, as well as typical text elements, such as italics, boldface type, sidebars, and captions.

The passages are stand-alone texts and can be used in any order you choose. Feel free to assign passages to individuals, pairs, small groups, or the entire class, as best suits your teaching style. However, it's a good idea to preview each passage before you assign it, to ensure that your students have the skills needed to complete it successfully. (See the next page for a close-reading routine to model for students.)

Reading-Comprehension Question Pages

Following each passage is a reproducible "Do More" page of text-dependent comprehension questions: two are multiple-choice questions that call for a single response and a brief, text-based explanation to justify that choice. The other two questions are open-response items. The questions address a range of comprehension strategies and skills. All questions share the goal of ensuring that students engage in close reading of the text, grasp its key ideas, and provide text-based evidence to support their answers. Have additional paper on hand so students have ample space to write complete and thorough answers.

An answer key (pages 54–63) includes annotated versions of each marked passage and sample answers to its related questions. Maintain flexibility in assessing student responses, as some markings and answers to open-response questions may vary. (Since students are likely to mark different places in the text as examples for particular skills, the annotated versions in the answer key highlight a variety of possible responses.) Encourage students to self-assess and revise their answers as you review the text markings together. This approach encourages discussion, comparison, extension, reinforcement, and correlation to other reading skills.

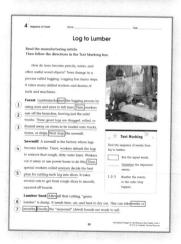

Teaching Routine for Close Reading and Purposeful Text Marking

Any text can become more accessible to readers who have learned to bring various strategies, such as purposeful text marking, to the reading process. Here is one suggested routine that may be effective in your classroom.

Preview

- **Engage prior knowledge** of the topic of the piece and its genre. Help students link it to similar topics or examples of the genre they may have read.

- **Identify the reading skill** for which students will be marking the text. Distribute the Comprehension Skill Summary Card that applies to the passage. Go over its key ideas. (See Comprehension Skill Summary Cards, page 8, for more.)

Model *(for the first passage, to familiarize students with the process)*

- **Display the passage,** using an interactive whiteboard, document camera, or other resource, and provide students with their own copy. Preview the text with students by having them read the title and look at any photographs, illustrations, or other graphics.

- **Draw attention to the markings** students will use to enhance their understanding of the piece. Link the text marking box to the Comprehension Skill Summary Card for clarification.

- **Read aloud the passage** as students follow along. Guide students to think about the skill and to note any questions they may have on sticky-notes.

- **Mark the text together.** Begin by numbering the paragraphs. Then discuss the choices you make when marking the text, demonstrating and explaining how the various text elements support the skill. Check that students understand how to mark the text using the various icons and graphics shown in the text marking box.

Read

- **Have students do a quick-read of the passage independently** for the gist. Then they should read it a second time, marking the text as they go.

- **Encourage students to make additional markings of their own.** These might include noting unfamiliar vocabulary, an idiom or phrase they may not understand, or an especially interesting, unusual, or important detail they want to remember. Invite them to use sticky-notes, colored pencils, highlighters, question marks, or check marks.

Respond

- **Have students read the passage a third time.** This reading should prepare them to discuss the piece and offer their views about it.

- **Have students answer the questions** on the companion Do More page. Encourage them to look back at their text markings and other text evidence. This will help students provide complete and supported responses.

Informational Passages for Text Marking & Close Reading: Grade 3
© 2015 by Scholastic Teaching Resources

Comprehension Skill Summary Cards

To help students review the ten reading-comprehension skills this book addresses and the specific terms associated with each, have them use the ten reproducible Comprehension Skill Summary Cards (pages 10–12). The boldface terms on each card are the same ones students will identify as they mark the text.

You might duplicate, cut out, and distribute a particular Comprehension Skill Summary Card before assigning a passage that focuses on that skill. Discuss the elements of the skill together to ensure that students fully grasp it. Encourage students to save and collect the cards, which they can use as a set of reading aids to refer to whenever they read any type of informational text.

Tips and Suggestions

- The text-marking process is versatile and adaptable. Although numbering, boxing, circling, and underlining are the most common methods, you can personalize the strategy for your class if it helps augment the process. You might have students use letters to mark text; they can, for example, write MI to indicate a main idea, D to mark a detail, or F for fact and O for opinion. Whichever technique you use, focus on the need for consistency of marking.

- You may wish to extend the text-marking strategy by having students identify other aspects of writing, such as figurative language or confusing words, expressions, or idioms. Moreover, you can invite students to write their own notes and questions in the margins.

Comprehension Skill

Main Idea & Details

Every passage has one or more main ideas supported by details. The main idea answers the question, "Who (or What) is this piece about?"

- The **main idea** is the most important point an author makes about a topic. The main idea in most paragraphs is stated in a *topic sentence*. The topic sentence can appear anywhere in a paragraph.

- **Supporting details** are facts, statements, examples, descriptions, and other information that tell more about the main idea.

Comprehension Skill

Sequence of Events

As you read, notice the order in which things happen or ideas are presented. Think about the *beginning, middle,* and *end.*

- **Events** are the important actions that happen.

- The **sequence** is the order in which events happen.

- **Signal words** give clues that help clarify the order of events. Examples include *first, second, third, next, then, last, later, before, prior to, soon, during, while, after, finally,* as well as specific dates and times.

Comprehension Skill

Compare & Contrast

Authors discuss people, places, objects, or ideas by describing how they are alike and ways they differ.

- To **compare** means to tell how two or more things are alike.

- To **contrast** means to tell how two or more things are different.

- **Signal words** guide you to compare and contrast.

Examples for comparing: *both, like, alike, also, too, share, in the same way,* and *similarly.*

Examples for contrasting: *but, only, unlike, instead, however, in contrast, different, although, on the other hand, as opposed to, neither, whereas, while,* and *rather.*

Connections to the Standards

The lessons in this book support the College and Career Readiness Anchor Standards for Reading for students in grades K–12. These broad standards, which serve as the basis of many state standards, were developed to establish rigorous educational expectations with the goal of providing students nationwide with a quality education that prepares them for college and careers. The chart below details how the lessons align with specific reading standards for informational text for students in grade 3.

These materials also address language standards, including skills in the conventions of standard English, knowledge of language, and vocabulary acquisition and use. In addition, students meet writing standards as they answer questions about the passages, demonstrating their ability to convey ideas coherently, clearly, and with support from the text.

Reading Standards for Informational Text	Passages
Key Ideas and Details	
• Ask and answer questions to demonstrate understanding of a text, referring explicitly to the text as the basis for the answers.	1–20
• Determine the main idea of a text; recount the key details and explain how they support the main idea.	1–20
• Describe the relationship between a series of historical events, scientific ideas or concepts, or steps in technical procedures in a text, using language that pertains to time, sequence, and cause/effect.	1–4, 7, 9–14, 16–20
Craft and Structure	
• Determine the meaning of general academic and domain-specific words or phrases in a text relevant to a grade 3 topic or subject area.	1–20
• Use text features and search tools (e.g., key words, sidebars, hyperlinks) to locate information relevant to a given topic efficiently.	1–4, 6–12, 14–17, 19, 20
Integration of Knowledge and Ideas	
• Use information gained from illustrations (e.g., maps, photographs) and words in a text to demonstrate understanding of the text (e.g., where, when, why, and how key events occur).	1–20
• Describe the logical connection between particular sentences and paragraphs in a text (e.g., comparison, cause/effect, first/second/third in a sequence).	1–20
Range of Reading and Level of Text Complexity	
• By the end of the year, read and comprehend informational texts, including history/social studies, science, and technical texts, at the high end of the grades 2–3 text complexity band independently and proficiently.	1–20

Source: © Copyright 2010 National Governors Association Center for Best Practices and Council of Chief State School Officers. All rights reserved.

Informational Passages for Text Marking & Close Reading: Grade 3
© 2015 by Scholastic Teaching Resources

Main Idea & Details

Every passage has one or more main ideas supported by details. The main idea answers the question, "Who (or What) is this piece about?"

- The **main idea** is the most important point an author makes about a topic. The main idea in most paragraphs is stated in a *topic sentence*. The topic sentence can appear anywhere in a paragraph.

- **Supporting details** are facts, statements, examples, descriptions, and other information that tell more about the main idea.

Sequence of Events

As you read, notice the order in which things happen or ideas are presented. Think about the *beginning*, *middle*, and *end*.

- **Events** are the important actions that happen.

- The **sequence** is the order in which events happen.

- **Signal words** give clues that help clarify the order of events. Examples include *first, second, third, next, then, last, later, before, prior to, soon, during, while, after, finally*, as well as specific dates and times.

Fact & Opinion

Do you truly *know* something or do you simply *believe* it? Telling the difference between knowing and believing is a critical reading and thinking skill.

- A **fact** is a statement you can prove or verify. Facts are true and certain.

- An **opinion** is a statement of personal belief or feeling. Opinions vary.

- **Signal words** can help you distinguish facts from opinions.

  Examples for facts: *proof, know,* and *discovered,* as well as details, such as dates and ages.

  Examples for opinions: *believe, wish, favor, expect, agree, disagree, probably, seems to, sense, think, viewpoint,* and *feel*.

Compare & Contrast

Authors discuss people, places, objects, or ideas by describing how they are alike and ways they differ.

- To **compare** means to tell how two or more things are alike.

- To **contrast** means to tell how two or more things are different.

- **Signal words** guide you to compare and contrast.

  Examples for comparing: *both, like, alike, also, too, share, in the same way,* and *similarly*.

  Examples for contrasting: *but, only, unlike, instead, however, in contrast, different, although, on the other hand, as opposed to, neither, whereas, while,* and *rather*.

Cause & Effect

A text may discuss the relationship between something that happens and any outcomes that follow from it.

- A **cause** is an event, condition, reason, or situation that makes something happen.

- An **effect** is the result of that particular event, condition, reason, or situation.

- **Signal words** are clues that help link a cause with its effects. Examples include *as a result, since, therefore, because of, so, for this reason, consequently, due to, so that, in order to,* and *leads to.*

Context Clues

Authors may use words you don't know. Search for synonyms, antonyms, explanations, or examples in the nearby text to help you figure out the meaning.

- **Context** refers to the words and sentences around the unfamiliar word.

- **Context clues** are specific indications in the text that can help you unlock the meaning of an unfamiliar word.

Problem & Solution

This kind of writing presents a challenging situation to engage readers, then offers one or more forms of resolution.

- A **problem** is a difficulty or setback situation that needs fixing.

- A **solution** is a way to deal with the problem to make things better.

- **Signal words** are clues that indicate a problem and its solutions.

  Examples for problems: *question, challenge, dilemma, issue, puzzle, need,* and *trouble.*

  Examples for solutions: *answer, result, one reason, solve, improve, fix, remedy, respond,* and *led to.*

Summarize

Think about how to retell the key ideas of a passage in your own words. Leave out unimportant details and get to the point.

- The **topic** is the focus of the passage— what it is mainly about.

- **Important details** add more information about the topic.

- A **summary** is a brief statement of the topic using its most essential details. A good summary is short, clear, and recalls what is most important.

Informational Passages for Text Marking & Close Reading: Grade 3
© 2015 by Scholastic Teaching Resources

Make Inferences

Authors may hint at an idea without stating it directly. You must use what you already know about a topic to "read between the lines" to figure out an unstated idea.

- **Text clues** are words or details that help you figure out unstated ideas.

- You **make an inference** by combining text clues with your background knowledge to come to a logical conclusion, or "educated guess."

Author's Purpose

Every author has goals in mind before writing. Close reading and common sense can help you figure out the author's intention.

- The **author's purpose** is the reason the author chose to write a particular piece. An author may write with more than one purpose.

- The main purposes for writing are to **inform** (tell, describe), to **persuade** (convince, influence), or to **entertain** (amuse, please).

- **Text clues** are words or sentences that reveal the author's purpose.

Informational Passages for Text Marking & Close Reading: Grade 3
© 2015 by Scholastic Teaching Resources

Informational
Text Passages

Teamwork on the Dance Floor

Read the dance article.
Then follow the directions in the Text Marking box.

Do you enjoy music and movement? Do you like being part of a group? If so, try square dancing. Square dancing is a form of folk dance. It's a casual type of dancing anybody can learn.

Square dancing began long ago in France. It was called the *quadrille* (kwa-DRILL). Four couples stood in a square; everyone faced the center. When musicians began to play, the *set* (a group of four couples) danced the moves they had learned ahead of time.

Children square dancing

Square dancers found much to like. They learned to mix musical rhythms with patterns of movement. They exercised their listening, thinking, and memory skills. They built cooperation and teamwork while having fun.

Square dancing eventually made its way to America. But nobody knows exactly how or when. People who knew the moves taught their friends so they could form sets. Over time, square dancing spread across America and became very popular.

People of all ages still square dance. Maybe there are square dancers in your community! Ask around.

Text Marking

Find the main idea
and supporting details.

◯ Circle the main idea
in each paragraph.

_____ Underline at least one
supporting detail for
each main idea.

Name _____   Date _____

Teamwork on the Dance Floor

▶ **Answer each question. Give evidence from the article.**

1 Which word has the same meaning as *set* (paragraph 2)?

○ A. group   ○ B. couple   ○ C. package   ○ D. scenery

What in the text helped you answer? _____

_____

_____

_____

2 What do you think the root word *quad* in *quadrille* means?

○ A. two   ○ B. leg muscles   ○ C. four   ○ D. dance muscles

What in the text helped you answer? _____

_____

_____

_____

3 Why is this kind of dancing called *square* dancing? Explain.

_____

_____

_____

_____

4 What things do square dancers enjoy?

_____

_____

_____

_____

Informational Passages for Text Marking & Close Reading: Grade 3
© 2015 by Scholastic Teaching Resources

Name _____ Date _____

Catch Me If You Can

Read the social studies article.
Then follow the directions in the Text Marking box.

Children all over the world enjoy running. This has been true throughout history. The pleasure of this kind of play eventually led to the creation of "chase" games. In these contests, one child would run from another to avoid being caught.

The names of chase games may have changed over time. But some of them are played today much like they were years ago.

<table>
<tr><td>

Text Marking

Find the main idea
and supporting details.

◯   Circle the main idea
         in each paragraph.

_____   Underline supporting
         details for each main idea.

</td></tr>
</table>

During the 1800s, *Hunt the Hare* was a popular chase game. In it, one child ran from another around the outside of a circle of players holding hands. The "hare" raced to avoid capture. One way to safety for the hare was to duck under the players' hands to get inside the circle. What game do you play today that reminds you of *Hunt the Hare*?

Other simple chase games were versions of the game we know as *Tag*. *Touch Wood* is an example. Runners in that game could escape being tagged by touching a tree or a fence. What kind of object might have saved a runner in *Touch Iron*?

Children playing a chase game in 1899

Informational Passages for Text Marking & Close Reading: Grade 3
© 2015 by Scholastic Teaching Resources

Name _____ Date _____

Catch Me If You Can

▶ **Answer each question. Give evidence from the article.**

1 Which of the following would also make a good title for this article?

  ◯ A. Games for Children   ◯ C. Chase Games Throughout History

  ◯ B. Hunt the Hare   ◯ D. Circle Games

What in the text helped you answer? _____

_____

_____

2 Which thing might a player tag for safety in a game of *Touch Iron*?

  ◯ A. an ironing board   ◯ C. a maple tree

  ◯ B. a chain-link fence   ◯ D. a rabbit

What in the text helped you answer? _____

_____

_____

3 Why have chase games always been popular?

_____

_____

_____

_____

4 Explain in your own words what *Hunt the Hare* and *Touch Wood* have in common.

_____

_____

_____

_____

The Giant Heart

Read the museum review.
Then follow the directions in the Text Marking box.

We entered the Franklin Institute right after it opened at 9:30 AM. Everyone in our class was excited. We were about to visit a heart—and not just any heart. This one is big enough for a person about as tall as the Statue of Liberty!

The first thing we noticed when we entered the exhibit hall was a sound. It was the lub-DUB of a heartbeat. We stood and listened. Then, we climbed up narrow steps to enter the heart itself.

There, we walked slowly from chamber to chamber. Within each enclosed space, there were science facts to read. First, we passed through a ventricle, one of the heart's lower chambers. Next, we crawled through an artery—a blood vessel that carries blood from the heart to the rest of the body. This artery was a tunnel eight feet long!

Exploring the Giant Heart

⭐ Text Marking

Find the sequence of events.

☐   Box the signal words.

_____   <u>Underline</u> the important events.

1-2-3   Number the events in the order they happened.

After exploring the Giant Heart we examined other displays about the heart. My favorite was the one that compared heart sizes of different animals.

I recommend this museum to anybody with a heart!

Informational Passages for Text Marking & Close Reading: Grade 3
© 2015 by Scholastic Teaching Resources

The Giant Heart

▶ **Answer each question. Give evidence from the review.**

1 Which is the best synonym for *chamber* (paragraph 3) as it is used in this review?

○ A. bedroom   ○ B. blood vessel   ○ C. enclosed space   ○ D. tunnel

What in the text helped you answer? _____

_____

_____

2 What did the class do after walking through the Giant Heart?

○ A. They visited the gift shop.

○ B. They crawled through an artery.

○ C. They listened to the heart beating.

○ D. They looked at other displays about hearts.

What in the text helped you answer? _____

_____

_____

3 What helped draw the students' attention to the Giant Heart?

_____

_____

_____

4 Think about your own heartbeat. Why do you think the writer wrote the sound as "lub-DUB"?

_____

_____

_____

Name _____ Date _____

Log to Lumber

Read the manufacturing article.
Then follow the directions in the Text Marking box.

How do trees become pencils, rulers, and other useful wood objects? Trees change in a process called logging. Logging has many steps. It takes many skilled workers and dozens of tools and machines.

Forest Lumberjacks start the logging process by using axes and saws to fell trees. Then, workers saw off the branches, leaving just the solid trunks. These giant logs are dragged, rolled, or floated away on rivers to be loaded onto trucks, trains, or ships. Next stop: the sawmill.

Sawmill A sawmill is the factory where logs become lumber. There, workers debark the logs to remove that rough, dirty outer layer. Workers cut it away or use power hoses to do this. Then, special workers called sawyers decide the best plan for cutting each log into slices. It takes several cuts to get from rough slices to smooth, squared-off boards.

Lumber Yard After all that cutting, "green lumber" is damp. It needs time, air, and heat to dry out. This can take weeks or months. Finally, the "seasoned" (dried) boards are ready to sell.

⭐ Text Marking ⭐

Find the sequence of events from log to lumber.

☐	Box the signal words.
_____	<u>Underline</u> the important events.
1-2-3	Number the events in the order they happen.

Informational Passages for Text Marking & Close Reading: Grade 3
© 2015 by Scholastic Teaching Resources

Log to Lumber

▶ **Answer each question. Give evidence from the article.**

1 Which is not another word for *wood*?

○ A. board   ○ B. lumber   ○ C. season   ○ D. timber

What in the text helped you answer? _____

_____

_____

2 Look at the photo. Which part of the logging process does it show?

○ A. hauling the logs   ○ C. deciding which tree to cut

○ B. selling seasoned boards   ○ D. rough-cutting at a sawmill

What in the text helped you answer? _____

_____

_____

_____

3 According to the article, what is *green lumber* (paragraph 4)?

_____

_____

_____

4 Notice that paragraphs 2, 3, and 4 begin with words in dark print. How do these clues help you better understand the logging process?

_____

_____

_____

_____

Name _____   Date _____

A Movie Classic

Read the personal anecdote.
Then follow the directions in the Text Marking box.

My mom believes that *The Wizard of Oz* is the best family movie ever. It came out in 1939. It was very popular. The American Film Institute has named it the #1 fantasy film.

I first saw this movie when I was six. That was my mom's age when she first saw it. She made me wait until then because, in her view, the scary scenes would frighten me.

We planned an Oz party. For "opening night," we made popcorn and sat on a yellow blanket—our Yellow Brick Road. Then mom hit PLAY.

To me, *The Wizard of Oz* began slowly and had boring parts. The Kansas scenes were in black and white. I preferred the scenes in colorful Oz. I enjoyed most of the songs and characters. But overall, I thought it was good, not great. The scary scenes didn't bother me. The tornado seemed like a carnival ride, and the Wicked Witch wasn't as mean as other movie witches I've seen. Still, I loved watching this famous film with my mom.

Text Marking

Identify the facts and opinions in the anecdote.

☐ Box at least three signal words or phrases.

◯ Circle at least three facts.

___ Underline at least three opinions.

Informational Passages for Text Marking & Close Reading: Grade 3
© 2015 by Scholastic Teaching Resources

A Movie Classic

▶ **Answer each question. Give evidence from the anecdote.**

1 Which of the following words means the opposite of *fantasy* (paragraph 1)?

○ A. familiar ○ B. favorite ○ C. fairy tale ○ D. reality

What in the text helped you answer? _____

_____

_____

2 Which clue tells you where the writer and his mom watched the movie?

○ A. Then mom hit PLAY.

○ B. I first saw this film when I was six.

○ C. The Kansas scenes were in black and white.

○ D. I loved watching this famous film with my mom.

What in the text helped you answer? _____

_____

_____

3 Summarize the writer's responses to seeing *The Wizard of Oz* for the first time.

_____

_____

_____

4 In your own words, explain how you could tell facts from opinions in this piece.

_____

_____

_____

Informational Passages for Text Marking & Close Reading: Grade 3
© 2015 by Scholastic Teaching Resources

Name _____

Date _____

Awesome Travel Experience

Read the travel ad.

Then follow the directions in the Text Marking box.

Are you ready for a jaw-dropping experience? Can you handle awesome beauty? If so, head to Niagara Falls. Here you will see one of North America's finest natural wonders. It's the best vacation spot for families, with much to do and see for folks of all ages.

Niagara Falls

In the Park Come visit America's oldest state park. Take fantastic photos. Hike marked trails through the park's 400 acres. Hungry? Our restaurants have tasty food and unforgettable views.

Above the Falls Soar over majestic Niagara Falls in a helicopter. You'll feel like an eagle. Or take in the dazzling fireworks on Friday and Saturday nights.

Text Marking

Identify the facts and opinions in the ad.

☐ Box at least three signal words or phrases.

◯ Circle at least three facts.

___ Underline at least three opinions.

Below the Falls Enjoy New York state's best boat cruise. Pass beside the thundering falls. See how 3,160 tons of tumbling water per second looks and feels close-up. Hear the mighty roar. Or take a misty but thrilling walk through Cave of the Winds. You can't get any nearer to the falls than that!

Come! We're certain you'll have the thrill of a lifetime!

Awesome Travel Experience

▶ **Answer each question. Give evidence from the ad.**

1 Which of the following experiences is most likely to be *jaw-dropping*? (paragraph 1)?

○ A. eating a tasty meal ○ C. watching puppies romp at a dog park

○ B. taking an action photograph ○ D. riding on a roller coaster

What in the text helped you answer? _____

_____

_____

2 Which of the following is a fact about Niagara Falls?

○ A. It is the best family vacation spot.

○ B. Its restaurants have unforgettable views.

○ C. There are fireworks on Friday and Saturday nights.

○ D. The Cave of the Winds walk is thrilling.

What in the text helped you answer? _____

_____

_____

3 Why do words in dark print begin three of the paragraphs in the ad?

_____

_____

_____

4 Why do you think ads like this one use words like *dazzling*, *fantastic*, and *thrilling*?

_____

_____

_____

Which Equine?

Read the nature article.
Then follow the directions in the Text Marking box.

Ponies are not baby horses, though people often think they are. In fact, horses and ponies are different animals in the same family. Both are *equines* (E-kwīnz). Let's compare them.

All equines are mammals. Horses and ponies are warm-blooded. They have backbones and skin covered with hair. Their babies are born live and nurse on the mother's milk. Both horses and ponies can be used for riding, doing farm work, or pulling wagons. Both graze to eat a plant-based diet. They enjoy hay, grass, leaves, fruits, vegetables, and oats.

But these two equines differ in several ways. The key contrast is in their heights. An equine is a horse if it's 58 or more inches tall at the shoulder. Ponies rarely get that tall. They have shorter legs, necks, and heads, and wider bodies than horses do. Ponies cope with cold weather better than horses do because they have thicker manes and coats.

Horses and ponies do not behave the same either. Both can be smart and stubborn, but ponies usually stay calmer than horses do.

Two full-grown equines—pony (left), horse (right)

Text Marking

Compare and contrast horses and ponies.

☐ Box at least three signal words or phrases.

◯ Circle at least three ways they are alike.

___ Underline at least three ways they are different.

Which Equine?

▶ **Answer each question. Give evidence from the article.**

1   1. Which of the following is not true about *mammals* (paragraph 2)?

    ○ A. They have hair.   ○ C. They are cold-blooded.

    ○ B. They have backbones.   ○ D. Their babies drink milk.

What in the text helped you answer? _____

_____

_____

2   Which is the most important way that horses and ponies are different?

    ○ A. Ponies have wider bodies than horses do.   ○ C. Ponies cannot pull wagons.

    ○ B. Ponies are shorter than horses.   ○ D. Horses do not eat plants.

What in the text helped you answer? _____

_____

_____

_____

3   In your own words, explain the difference between a pony and a baby horse.

_____

_____

_____

_____

4   Why don't horses cope as well in cold weather as ponies do?

_____

_____

Name _____ Date _____

Shopping for Skates

Read the sports article.

Then follow the directions in the Text Marking box.

Anyone can learn to ice skate. All you need is a safe, smooth, icy surface and skates. But which kind of skates should you pick? There are two main choices: hockey skates or figure skates. They differ in their boots and blades.

Boots All ice skates have steel blades attached to the bottoms of boots. Both types of boots lace up the front. Figure-skating boots are made of sturdy, long-lasting leather with thin linings. They give ankle support to skaters for jumps and turns. By contrast, hockey boots are now made of hard plastic with padded linings for protection and comfort.

Blades The blades differ, too. Hockey blades are shorter and narrower than figure-skate blades. This helps hockey players skate fast and quickly change direction. Figure-skating blades are longer and heavier for smooth gliding on ice. Only figure-skate blades have a "toe pick" at the front. This jagged section helps skaters dig into the ice to jump.

Hockey skates

Figure skates

⭐ Text Marking

Compare and contrast hockey and figure skates.

☐	Box at least three signal words or phrases.
⬭	Circle two ways they are alike.
___	Underline at least three ways they are different.

Informational Passages for Text Marking & Close Reading: Grade 3
© 2015 by Scholastic Teaching Resources

Name _____ Date _____

Shopping for Skates

▶ **Answer each question. Give evidence from the article.**

1 Which word from the article means "built well to last through hard use"?

◯ A. sturdy ◯ B. padded ◯ C. jagged ◯ D. thin

What in the text helped you answer? _____

_____

_____

2 Which is a way that figure skates and hockey skates are alike?

◯ A. Both have toe picks. ◯ C. Both have padded linings.

◯ B. Both have steel blades. ◯ D. Both can be worn to play hockey.

What in the text helped you answer? _____

_____

_____

3 In your own words, explain why figure skates and hockey skates are made differently.

_____

_____

_____

_____

4 Look at the skates in the photos. What differences can you see that are not mentioned in the text? Use another sheet of paper if you need more space.

_____

_____

_____

Informational Passages for Text Marking & Close Reading: Grade 3
© 2015 by Scholastic Teaching Resources

Name _____ Date _____

Avalanche!

Read the earth science essay.
Then follow the directions in the Text Marking box.

Have you ever watched how snow behaves on a car's windshield? If the temperature stays low, the snow sticks. But if the temperature rises, the snow begins to slide. It moves in chunks down the windshield.

This is a tiny example of an avalanche— a sudden surge of snow and ice down a mountain. A large avalanche might let loose enough snow to cover 20 soccer fields 10-feet deep!

Roaring Snowball Avalanches occur when piled-up layers of snow get too heavy and then weaken. The loosened snow starts to slide down. As it speeds up, it picks up rocks, trees, and even houses, animals, and people in its path. Avalanches grow in size, affecting everything in their way.

Text Marking

Find the causes and effects of an avalanche.

☐ Box at least three signal words or phrases.

◯ Circle the causes.

___ Underline the effects.

Causes Many factors can set off an avalanche. Some are natural causes: heavy rains, warming temperatures, earthquakes, or changes in wind direction. And then there are human causes: snowmobiling, skiing, or explosions.

Danger! Avalanches generally occur in winter or spring. But they can happen any time. And because they start so suddenly, they can be very dangerous.

Avalanche!

► **Answer each question. Give evidence from the essay.**

1 Which of the following words means the same as *factors* (paragraph 4)?

○ A. dangers   ○ B. seasons   ○ C. causes   ○ D. layers

What in the text helped you answer? _____

_____

_____

2 According to the essay, which of the following does not cause avalanches?

○ A. mountain height   ○ B. snowmobiling   ○ C. earthquakes   ○ D. heavy rains

What in the text helped you answer? _____

_____

_____

_____

3 Why are avalanches so dangerous?

_____

_____

_____

_____

4 Why do you think the author begins the essay by describing how snow acts on a car's windshield?

_____

_____

_____

_____

Informational Passages for Text Marking & Close Reading:
© 2015 by Scholastic Teaching Resources

Name _____ Date _____

Traffic Jam

Read the current events article.
Then follow the directions in the Text Marking box.

When the president visits a crowded big city like Boston or Chicago, many residents feel the effects. The president is in our city, New York, today. He is here to give a speech. So the city is on high alert. Police are out in force to provide added safety.

The president's motorcade in New York City

Due to the president's visit, some major streets are closed entirely. Others have lanes blocked. Some bus routes are changed. Traffic snarls to a standstill in some places. Pedestrians and drivers alike are affected. As a result, people trying to get around by foot or car get stuck.

Because of the clogged roads, most cars, trucks, cabs, and buses take much longer to get where they are going. Imagine how annoying this is for busy people just trying to go about their normal lives! As streets turn into parking lots, more people choose to go underground. There they can travel more quickly by subway.

After the president leaves town, streets will open up, the traffic will flow naturally, and life will return to normal.

★ Text Marking ★

Find the causes and effects in the article.

☐ Box at least three signal words or phrases.

◯ Circle the causes.

___ Underline the effects.

Traffic Jam

▶ **Answer each question. Give evidence from the article.**

1 How do *pedestrians* (paragraph 2) get around town?

○ A. by flying   ○ B. by riding   ○ C. by driving   ○ D. by walking

What in the text helped you answer? _____

_____

_____

2 Which of the following is *not* an effect of traffic jams?

○ A. The president comes to town.   ○ C. People get annoyed.

○ B. Travel choices may change.   ○ D. Travel takes longer.

Explain your answer. _____

_____

_____

3 What does the author mean by writing that "…streets turn into parking lots"?

_____

_____

_____

4 In your own words, explain how a visit by the president affects travel in a busy city.

_____

_____

_____

_____

Informational Passages for Text Marking & Close Reading: Grade 3
© 2015 by Scholastic Teaching Resources

Name _____ Date _____

Name That Landform

Read the geography essay.
Then follow the directions in the Text Marking box.

The landscape changes as you drive across America from east to west. In the middle of the country, you see *prairie*—rolling or level grassland with few trees. Prairie land is good for farming and ranching.

As you drive farther west, the land rises. You see many interesting shapes called landforms. These shapes are made of rock and dirt. Each landform has its own name, based on its shape and features.

A *plateau* (pla-TOE) is one kind of landform. It is vast in area and higher than the land around it. A plateau is mostly level, with at least one steep side. Plateaus exist all over the world.

Mesa (MAY-sa) is the Spanish word for "table." A mesa is a high landform, smaller than a plateau, with a flat top and steep sides. A *butte* (byoot) is a lone hill or mountain. It is smaller than a mesa. A butte has steep sides and either a flat or rounded top. The top of a butte is much smaller than the top of a mesa.

Text Marking

Use context clues to unlock word meanings.

◯ Circle the words *prairie*, *plateau*, *mesa*, and *butte* (the first time you read them).

_____ Underline context clues for each word.

Informational Passages for Text Marking & Close Reading: Grade 3
© 2015 by Scholastic Teaching Resources

Name _____   Date _____

Name That Landform

▶ **Answer each question. Give evidence from the essay.**

1 Which word can replace *vast* in paragraph 3 without changing the meaning of the sentence?

  ○ A. west   ○ B. steep   ○ C. huge   ○ D. lone

What in the text helped you answer? _____

_____

_____

2 Which of the following is not a landform?

  ○ A. tree   ○ B. mesa   ○ C. butte   ○ D. mountain

What in the text helped you answer? _____

_____

_____

3 Review the landforms described in the essay. Which might be the best place to grow crops? Explain your answer.

_____

_____

_____

4 Look at the photos. Which is the butte? Which is the mesa? How do you know?

_____

_____

_____

_____

_____

Informational Passages for Text Marking & Close Reading: Grade 3

Name _____   Date _____

Fascinating Frogs

Read the life science article.
Then follow the directions in the Text Marking box.

In the fairy tale *The Frog Prince*, an ugly frog kisses a princess and then turns into a handsome prince. They marry and live happily ever after. In real life, frogs don't kiss princesses, but they are otherwise remarkable animals.

Frogs are amphibians. All amphibians are cold-blooded—their bodies have the same temperature as the air or water they live in. Amphibians have backbones, no scales, and moist skin. Frogs begin their lives in calm water as eggs and then as tadpoles.

But that just defines frogs. What is interesting is that there are more than 6,300 species of frog! Some are as small as flies, while others are big enough to eat small snakes, mice, and other frogs. Some frogs can jump 10 feet. Some live more than 20 years.

Also interesting is how long frogs have been around. Herpetologists (HUR-puh-tol-oh-jists)—the scientists who study amphibians and snakes—know that frogs have existed for at least 200 million years! They were here along with the dinosaurs.

European tree frog

★ Text Marking ★

Use context clues to unlock word meanings.

 Circle the words *amphibians* and *herpetologists* (the first time you read them).

 Underline context clues for each word.

Informational Passages for Text Marking & Close Reading: Grade 3
© 2015 by Scholastic Teaching Resources

Name _____ Date _____

Fascinating Frogs

▶ **Answer each question. Give evidence from the article.**

1 Which of the following has the same meaning as *moist* (paragraph 2)?

○ A. dry   ○ B. damp   ○ C. scaly   ○ D. lumpy

What in the text helped you answer? _____

_____

_____

2 Which of the following is *not* true about frogs?

○ A. They have scales.   ○ C. Young frogs are called tadpoles.

○ B. They have backbones.   ○ D. Frogs have been around for millions of years.

What in the text helped you answer? _____

_____

_____

_____

3 How do you know that frogs are cold-blooded?

_____

_____

_____

_____

4 Why do you think the author began this article by describing a fairy tale?

_____

_____

_____

_____

Informational Passages for Text Marking & Close Reading: Grade 3
© 2015 by Scholastic Teaching Resources

Name _____ Date _____

Musical Memory

Read the music article.
Then follow the directions in the Text Marking box.

Musicians enjoy performing. Learning to play correctly takes time and effort. To perform well, musicians must learn every note, when to play loudly or softly, quickly or slowly, and when to pause. But that is not enough.

The best musicians believe that performing from memory gets the best results. Memorizing music sounds very hard. But there is a proven answer: practice, practice, practice!

Before trying to memorize any piece, learn to play it as written. Follow any method your music teacher suggests. Practice until you can play the whole piece perfectly.

Now focus on memorizing. This takes time, but it works. Start small. Focus on short sections, such as a line or two of music. Repeat three times without error. Continue until you can do this without looking at the music. Muscles remember what you practice.

Next, memorize longer chunks, such as a full page. Repeat without error again and again to train your brain and muscles to know just what to do. The problem of memorizing a piece disappears. You're ready to perform!

★ Text Marking

Find the problem musicians face and the solutions.

☐ Box the signal words.

◯ Circle the problem.

__ Underline the solutions.

Name _____ Date _____

Musical Memory

▶ **Answer each question. Give evidence from the article.**

1 *Memorizing* music means learn to _____.

○ A. read it   ○ B. practice it   ○ C. play it by heart   ○ D. play an instrument

What in the text helped you answer? _____

_____

_____

2 What must you do before you memorize a piece of music?

○ A. Tune your instrument.   ○ C. Sing the piece to yourself.

○ B. Join a band or orchestra.   ○ D. Learn the piece perfectly, note by note.

What in the text helped you answer? _____

_____

_____

3 Explain how practice helps to train the muscles of a musician.

_____

_____

_____

_____

4 In your own words, summarize how to memorize a piece of music.

_____

_____

_____

_____

_____

Informational Passages for Text Marking & Close Reading: Grade 3
© 2015 by Scholastic Teaching Resources

Name _____ Date _____

Work Wear

Read the historical anecdote.
Then follow the directions in the Text Marking box.

In 1849, gold was discovered in California. Men from far and wide flocked there to seek their fortunes. Business people followed the "forty-niners" to sell them clothing, supplies, and mining gear. Levi Strauss was one of these people. He arrived in California in 1853 to sell fabric and other goods.

In those days, work was as hard on clothing as it was on people. It was a problem for workers to get sturdy clothing that would last.

A solution arose in 1872, when Strauss got a letter from Jacob Davis. Davis was a tailor who had bought fabric from him. He used *rivets* instead of just thread to hold pants together in a better way. Davis thought rivets could make pants last longer, but he wanted Strauss's help. The men became partners.

On May 20, 1873, Levi Strauss and Jacob Davis got a *patent*. This legal paper gave them the right to make and sell riveted work pants. And so they did. Their "waist overalls"—the very first blue jeans—were a hit. Rivets made all the difference.

An old Levi Strauss advertisement

Text Marking

Find the problem workers faced.
Find the solution.

☐ Box the signal words.

◯ Circle the problem.

___ Underline the solution.

rivet: short metal fastener more long-lasting than thread

Name _____ Date _____

Work Wear

▶ **Answer each question. Give evidence from the anecdote.**

1 What does it mean that men *flocked* to California to seek their fortunes (paragraph 1)?

○ A. The men went one by one. ○ C. The men flew there in airplanes.

○ B. The men went in great numbers. ○ D. The men traveled in a V-form, as birds do.

What in the text helped you answer? _____

_____

_____

2 What product made Levi Strauss famous to this day?

○ A. denim fabric ○ B. miner's shovels ○ C. sturdy work pants ○ D. rivets

What in the text helped you answer? _____

_____

_____

3 Look at the picture. What makes it a good ad for Strauss's product?

_____

_____

_____

_____

4 Make an inference. Why did Levi Strauss and Jacob Davis make a successful team?

_____

_____

_____

_____

_____

Name _____ Date _____

L-o-n-g Sandwiches

Read the word origin article.
Then follow the directions in the Text Marking box.

Have you seen those oversized sandwiches that are popular at parties? Picture a long roll stuffed with meat, cheese, and veggies. Some gigantic versions can be 10-feet long. Those monsters are carried on a board so they hold their shape.

Any sandwich as massive as these deserves its own name. But the truth is, sandwiches like these have many names. The ones you know probably depend on where you live.

Linguists know that one thing can have many different names. This is true for the long stuffed sandwich. Some people call them hero sandwiches, maybe because it would take a superhero to finish one! Others call them subs, torpedoes, or tunnels. Those names suggest their shape. Other names include grinders, hoagies, or wedges.

Few facts prove which name came first or how, where, and why the names arose. So don't worry so much about the name. Just enjoy the taste. And don't forget napkins!

Text Marking

Summarize the text.

◯ Circle the topic.

_____ <u>Underline</u> important details.

---

linguist: a person who studies language and how it changes

Informational Passages for Text Marking & Close Reading: Grade 3
© 2015 by Scholastic Teaching Resources

Name _____ Date _____

L-o-n-g Sandwiches

▶ **Answer each question. Give evidence from the article.**

1 The word *massive* (paragraph 2) means _____.

○ A. delicious   ○ B. enormous   ○ C. fearless   ○ D. popular

What in the text helped you answer? _____

_____

_____

2 Which of the following would make another good title for this article?

○ A. Any Number of Names   ○ C. Linguists at Work

○ B. Supper for Superheroes   ○ D. Food for Thought

What in the text helped you answer? _____

_____

_____

3 Look back at your text markings. Write a short summary of this article.

_____

_____

_____

_____

_____

4 In paragraph 1, why does the author refer to some sandwiches as *monsters*?

_____

_____

_____

Informational Passages for Text Marking & Close Reading: Grade 3
© 2015 by Scholastic Teaching Resources

Name _____ Date _____

Puppets That Dance on Water

Read the cultural arts essay.
Then follow the directions in the Text Marking box.

A puppet is a kind of doll moved by hand. Somebody who performs this work is called a puppeteer. Puppets can be made from all kinds of materials and are often used to amuse or teach.

Puppetry is an art form in many cultures. Vietnam is a long, narrow country in southeast Asia, near China. Vietnam borders the sea. Its long tradition of puppetry goes back almost 1,000 years. One form is called *mua roi nuroc*, which means "puppets that dance on water." This is exactly what they appear to do.

Water puppets on a dragon boat

Water puppets are carved of wood and then painted. Each puppet is supported by a long rod hidden under the water. Puppeteers pull strings and wires to make the parts of a puppet move. The stage is a pool of water several feet deep. The puppeteers stand in the water behind a screen to work the puppets.

Water puppet shows are usually held at outdoor festivals. Musicians play as the puppets act out folktales, myths, or stories about village life.

Text Marking

Summarize the text.

⬭ Circle the topic.

_____ Underline important details.

Name _____ Date _____

Puppets That Dance on Water

▶ **Answer each question. Give evidence from the essay.**

1 Another word for *amuse* (paragraph 1) is _____.

○ A. dance   ○ B. entertain   ○ C. frighten   ○ D. paint

What in the text helped you answer? _____

_____

_____

2 What material is used to make the Vietnamese water puppets?

○ A. any kind of material   ○ B. string and wires   ○ C. wood   ○ D. paper

What in the text helped you answer? _____

_____

_____

3 Look back at your text markings. Write a short summary of the information given in the essay.

_____

_____

_____

_____

_____

4 Look at the photo. What kind of story might those water puppets be telling?

_____

_____

_____

_____

Informational Passages for Text Marking & Close Reading: Grade 3
© 2015 by Scholastic Teaching Resources

"Why Not?"

Read the biographical sketch.
Then follow the directions in the Text Marking box.

Lonnie Johnson always loved taking things apart. Sometimes he put them back together. Other times, he combined odd parts to make new things. He learned how to use tools from his dad.

At 13, Lonnie put an old engine on a homemade go-cart. He loved zooming around in it. He dreamed of being an inventor.

By high school, Lonnie built a remote-control robot from junk. This won him first prize at the Alabama State Science Fair. His friends called him "The Professor." In college, Lonnie was an honor student. Later, he became an Air Force officer, rocket scientist, and business leader. But he never stopped inventing.

You may have played with his most famous invention—the Super Soaker®. Lonnie got the idea for this power-squirt toy while working on another invention. When he tested a homemade part in his bathroom, it shot water across the room.

Today, Dr. Lonnie Johnson has more than 100 successful inventions. He remains curious and keeps trying new things.

Dr. Lonnie Johnson in his lab

★ ★ Text Marking ★ ★

Make an inference: What helped Dr. Lonnie Johnson reach his dream?

_____ <u>Underline</u> text clues.

Think about what you already know.

Informational Passages for Text Marking & Close Reading: Grade 3
© 2015 by Scholastic Teaching Resources

Name _____ Date _____

"Why Not?"

▶ **Answer each question. Give evidence from the biographical sketch.**

1 Make an inference. Why do you think Lonnie Johnson's high school friends called him "The Professor"?

- ○ A. They thought he was brave.
- ○ B. They thought he loved college.
- ○ C. They thought he was very smart.
- ○ D. They thought he acted older than they did.

What in the text helped you answer? _____

_____

_____

2 Based on the piece, Lonnie Johnson invented the Super Soaker® _____.

- ○ A. by accident
- ○ B. for his children
- ○ C. for a science fair
- ○ D. to produce clean energy

What in the text helped you answer? _____

_____

_____

3 Reread the title. When someone told Lonnie Johnson that an idea would never work, he gave those two words as his answer. What does this tell you about him?

_____

_____

_____

4 Look back at your text markings. Think about what you already know. How did Dr. Johnson reach his dream? Use another sheet of paper if you need more space.

_____

_____

Name _____ Date _____

Food for Thought

Read the nutrition article.
Then follow the directions in the Text Marking box.

Does it matter how much fat, salt, and sugar children eat? Should kids avoid fatty foods like chicken fingers and French fries? Should they steer clear of salty junk foods, like puffed cheese sticks? Should they stay away from foods loaded with chemicals and dyes? Soda has both.

A healthy salad

Fat, salt, and sugar make foods taste good. But too much of a good thing can harm you. That's why food scientists strongly support healthy eating. They want to direct children and parents toward wiser food choices. Teachers, school nurses, doctors, and many parents agree. They hope schools will share the responsibility of keeping kids fit and strong.

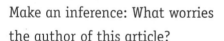

Text Marking

Make an inference: What worries the author of this article?

_____ <u>Underline</u> text clues.

 Think about what you already know.

So, many school communities urge cafeteria lunches to be both tasty *and* nourishing. They encourage serving wholesome, natural foods. They don't want kids eating foods with unhealthy ingredients in them. And scientists and educators want school lunches to be varied. They suggest that menus celebrate cultural differences.

Teachers and principals care deeply about how kids learn best. Science shows that a healthy diet increases a child's ability to stay alert for learning. That is surely food for thought.

Informational Passages for Text Marking & Close Reading: Grade 3
© 2015 by Scholastic Teaching Resources

Food for Thought

▶ **Answer each question. Give evidence from the article.**

1 Foods with too much sugar, fat, or salt are called _____.

○ A. junk foods   ○ B. sandwiches   ○ C. school food   ○ D. wholesome choices

What in the text helped you answer? _____

_____   _____

_____

2 Which word means the same as *steer clear* (paragraph 1)?

○ A. encourage   ○ B. direct   ○ C. avoid   ○ D. vary

What in the text helped you answer? _____

_____

_____

3 Look back at your text markings. Think about what you already know. What does the writer think about how kids eat?

_____

_____

_____

_____

_____

4 Why would educators support wholesome school lunches?

_____

_____

_____

_____

As Fit as a Clown

Read the physical education article.
Then follow the directions in the Text Marking box.

Are you "circus fit"? Big-top performers are. They need to be in peak condition. How else could they perform all those wacky stunts? How do they juggle while balancing on a rope? How do they ride around backwards on a unicycle?

To do all this nutty stuff, circus performers exercise a lot. They must be as strong as they are silly. They must be as fit as they are funny. One major circus now shares its fitness secrets with kids. Clowns, dancers, and acrobats visit schools to teach what they do to stay in shape.

Kids who take part may not learn to prance about in huge flapping shoes. But they will learn how to be strong and flexible. They will get tips for keeping fit and staying safe. Plus, they may learn riddles like this one:

Q: Why do lions like to eat high-wire artists?

A: Because they want a well-balanced meal!

When that circus comes to town, the kids get to attend. Some lucky ones may even step into the ring and perform!

Text Marking

Check to identify the author's <u>two</u> purposes in this article.

☐ to entertain (E)

☐ to inform (I)

☐ to persuade (P)

_____ <u>Underline</u> text clues for this purpose. Write E, I, or P in the margin beside each clue.

As Fit as a Clown

▶ **Answer each question. Give evidence from the article.**

1 Which person below must be in *peak condition* (paragraph 1) for his or her job?

○ A. a librarian   ○ C. a school nurse

○ B. a bank teller   ○ D. a professional athlete

What in the text helped you answer? _____

_____

_____

2 Based on the article, what do circus performers teach when they visit schools?

○ A. how to walk on a high wire   ○ C. how to exercise to build strength

○ B. how to put on clown makeup   ○ D. how to twirl plates on a long stick

What in the text helped you answer? _____

_____

_____

3 Reread the riddle. What makes it funny? Why did the author include it?

_____

_____

_____

4 Review your text markings for author's purpose. Summarize why the author wrote this article. Use another sheet of paper if you need more space.

_____

_____

_____

_____

A Pool in Every School

Read the letter to the editor.
Then follow the directions in the Text Marking box.

To the Editor:

    We citizens expect our schools to be well equipped. We make sure that our children have classrooms supplied with the latest technology and the most effective educational equipment. We also favor having organized and well-outfitted athletics programs, from soccer to gymnastics. But shouldn't our schools provide one more kind of training for our students: a swimming program?

    Every child should learn how to swim. Swimming improves fitness and health. Swimmers develop strong muscles. Plus, swimming is a lifetime pleasure. It's so enjoyable to leap from a dock into a still lake or glide down a winding water slide into a welcoming pool. And snorkeling or diving underwater to see colorful fish and beautiful coral is a blast!

Text Marking

Check to identify the author's purpose in this letter.

[ ] to entertain (E)

[ ] to inform (I)

[ ] to persuade (P)

_____ <u>Underline</u> text clues for this purpose. Write E, I, or P in the margin beside each clue.

    But there is a more important reason why all kids should become good swimmers: safety in water. For that key reason alone, our schools should teach students to swim.

    So I urge all schools to offer swimming instruction—for fun, for fitness, and for safety. Let's put a pool in every school!

Nora Liu

El Paso, TX

A Pool in Every School

▶ **Answer each question. Give evidence from the letter to the editor.**

1 If a classroom is *well equipped* (paragraph 1), it has _____.

○ A. matching uniforms for students

○ B. different kinds of student teams

○ C. enough desks and chairs for everyone

○ D. plenty of books, computers, and teaching tools

What in the text helped you answer? _____

_____

2 Which is *not* a reason the author gives for having a swimming program in school?

○ A. Students who swim do better in school.

○ B. Knowing how to swim can save lives.

○ C. The ability to swim can be a lot of fun.

○ D. Swimming is a healthy activity.

What in the text helped you answer? _____

_____

3 Is Liu's idea to put a pool in every school practical? Why or why not?

_____

_____

_____

_____

4 Look back at your text markings. Summarize the author's purpose for writing this letter. Write your answer on another sheet of paper.

Informational Passages for Text Marking & Close Reading: Grade 3
© 2015 by Scholastic Teaching Resources

Answer Key

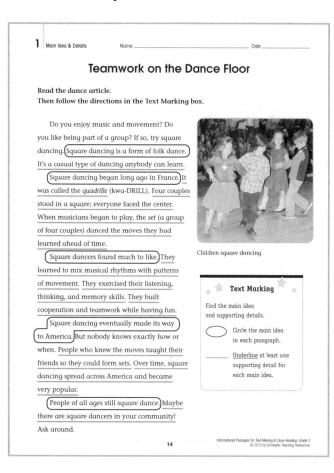

◀ Sample Text Markings

Passage 1: Teamwork on the Dance Floor

1. A; Sample answer: The sentence it's used in says that a set is a group of four couples.

2. C; Sample answer: In paragraph 2, it says that a *quadrille* was an early form of square dancing in which four couples stood in a square.

3. Sample answer: It is called square dancing because the eight people (four couples) in the set begin by standing and facing each other to form a square shape.

4. Sample answer: Paragraph 3 says that square dancers learn to mix music and patterns of movement. They exercise skills like listening, and work as a team while having fun.

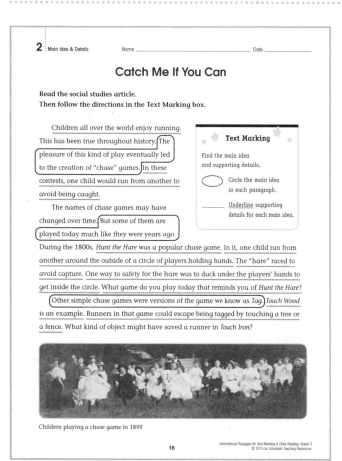

◀ Sample Text Markings

Passage 2: Catch Me If You Can

1. C; Sample answer: I picked C because it goes with the main idea of the whole article. The others titles are more like details from it.

2. B; Sample answer: A chain-link fence is the only choice that is made of iron (or another metal).

3. Sample answer: Children have always loved to run, so making running a part of a game made sense. And they didn't need any special equipment.

4. Sample answer: Both are chase games that involve running away from someone who wants to catch you.

Informational Passages for Text Marking & Close Reading: Grade 3
© 2015 by Scholastic Teaching Resources

3 Sequence of Events   Name _____ Date _____

The Giant Heart

Read the museum review.
Then follow the directions in the Text Marking box.

(1) We entered the Franklin Institute [right after] it opened at [9:30 A.M.] Everyone in our class was excited. We were [about to] visit a heart—and not just any heart. This one is big enough for a person about as tall as the Statue of Liberty!

(2) [The first thing] we noticed when we entered the exhibit hall was a sound. It was the lub-DUB of a heartbeat. We stood and listened. [Then,] we climbed up

(3) narrow steps to enter the heart itself.

(4) There, we walked slowly from chamber to chamber. Within each enclosed space, there were science

(5) facts to read. [First,] we passed through a ventricle, one of the heart's lower

(6) chambers. [Next,] we crawled through an artery—a blood vessel that carries blood from the heart to the rest of the body. This artery was a tunnel eight feet long!

(7) [After] exploring the Giant Heart we examined other displays about the heart. My favorite was the one that compared heart sizes of different animals.

I recommend this museum to anybody with a heart!

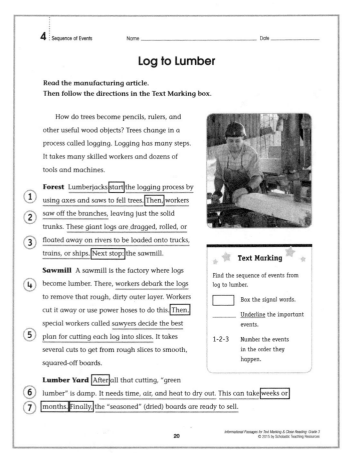

Exploring the Giant Heart

★ **Text Marking** ★

Find the sequence of events.

☐ Box the signal words.

___ Underline the important events.

1-2-3 Number the events in the order they happened.

18

Informational Passages for Text Marking & Close Reading: Grade 3
© 2015 by Scholastic Teaching Resources

Passage 3: The Giant Heart

1. C; Sample answer: The next sentence uses the words "enclosed space," which is a clue.

2. D; Sample answer: In the fourth paragraph, the writer says they did this.

3. Sample answer: The first thing they noticed was the loud heartbeat sounds.

4. Sample answer: My heart feels like it beats in a pattern of a soft lub and then a harder DUB. So that might be what the author meant.

---

4 Sequence of Events   Name _____ Date _____

Log to Lumber

Read the manufacturing article.
Then follow the directions in the Text Marking box.

How do trees become pencils, rulers, and other useful wood objects? Trees change in a process called logging. Logging has many steps. It takes many skilled workers and dozens of tools and machines.

Forest Lumberjacks [start] the logging process by

(1) using axes and saws to fell trees. [Then,] workers

(2) saw off the branches, leaving just the solid trunks. These giant logs are dragged, rolled, or

(3) floated away on rivers to be loaded onto trucks, trains, or ships. [Next stop:] the sawmill.

Sawmill A sawmill is the factory where logs

(4) become lumber. There, workers debark the logs to remove that rough, dirty outer layer. Workers cut it away or use power hoses to do this. [Then,]

(5) special workers called sawyers decide the best plan for cutting each log into slices. It takes several cuts to get from rough slices to smooth, squared-off boards.

Lumber Yard [After] all that cutting, "green

(6) lumber" is damp. It needs time, air, and heat to dry out. This can take [weeks or]

(7) [months.] Finally, the "seasoned" (dried) boards are ready to sell.

★ **Text Marking** ★

Find the sequence of events from log to lumber.

☐ Box the signal words.

___ Underline the important events.

1-2-3 Number the events in the order they happen.

20

Informational Passages for Text Marking & Close Reading: Grade 3
© 2015 by Scholastic Teaching Resources

Passage 4: Log to Lumber

1. C; Sample answer: All the other words are used to describe wood at different times in the logging process.

2. D; Sample answer: I can see that the bark has been cut off and the log has been squared off but not yet cut into boards, so I think it shows the part at the sawmill.

3. Sample answer: Green lumber is wood cut from a log into boards, but it's still too damp to sell. It needs time to dry out.

4. Sample answer: They help break down the different parts of the process and let me know that it happens in different places.

A Movie Classic

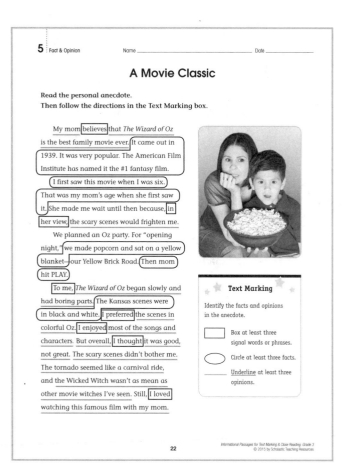

5 Fact & Opinion   Name _____   Date _____

A Movie Classic

Read the personal anecdote.
Then follow the directions in the Text Marking box.

My mom believes that *The Wizard of Oz* is the best family movie ever. It came out in 1939. It was very popular. The American Film Institute has named it the #1 fantasy film.

I first saw this movie when I was six. That was my mom's age when she first saw it. She made me wait until then because, in her view, the scary scenes would frighten me.

We planned an Oz party. For "opening night," we made popcorn and sat on a yellow blanket—our Yellow Brick Road. Then mom hit PLAY.

To me, *The Wizard of Oz* began slowly and had boring parts. The Kansas scenes were in black and white. I preferred the scenes in colorful Oz. I enjoyed most of the songs and characters. But overall, I thought it was good, not great. The scary scenes didn't bother me. The tornado seemed like a carnival ride, and the Wicked Witch wasn't as mean as other movie witches I've seen. Still, I loved watching this famous film with my mom.

Text Marking

Identify the facts and opinions in the anecdote.

☐ Box at least three signal words or phrases.

⬭ Circle at least three facts.

<u>Underline</u> at least three opinions.

22

Informational Passages for Text Marking & Close Reading: Grade 3
© 2015 by Scholastic Teaching Resources

Passage 5: A Movie Classic

1. D; Sample answer: The movie is about a place called Oz with a wicked witch. I know it is an imaginary place—not a real place.

2. A; Sample answer: That sentence tells me that they watched at home with a DVD player or on a computer. You don't hit PLAY in a movie theater!

3. Sample answer: The writer expected a great movie, but found it a bit disappointing. It wasn't as scary as expected, and it had boring parts. To the writer, the best parts were the music and watching with his mom.

4. Sample answer: Facts are statements that are true or really happened. But opinions are how someone feels. Also, there are signal words that are clues, like "to me," "I preferred," and "I loved," which I put boxes around.

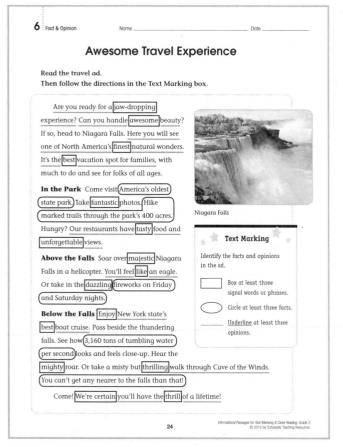

6 Fact & Opinion   Name _____   Date _____

Awesome Travel Experience

Read the travel ad.
Then follow the directions in the Text Marking box.

Are you ready for a jaw-dropping experience? Can you handle awesome beauty? If so, head to Niagara Falls. Here you will see one of North America's finest natural wonders. It's the best vacation spot for families, with much to do and see for folks of all ages.

In the Park Come visit America's oldest state park. Take fantastic photos. Hike marked trails through the park's 400 acres. Hungry? Our restaurants have tasty food and unforgettable views.

Above the Falls Soar over majestic Niagara Falls in a helicopter. You'll feel like an eagle. Or take in the dazzling fireworks on Friday and Saturday nights.

Below the Falls Enjoy New York state's best boat cruise. Pass beside the thundering falls. See how 3,160 tons of tumbling water per second looks and feels close-up. Hear the mighty roar. Or take a misty but thrilling walk through Cave of the Winds. You can't get any nearer to the falls than that!

Come! We're certain you'll have the thrill of a lifetime!

Niagara Falls

Text Marking

Identify the facts and opinions in the ad.

☐ Box at least three signal words or phrases.

⬭ Circle at least three facts.

<u>Underline</u> at least three opinions.

24

Informational Passages for Text Marking & Close Reading: Grade 3
© 2015 by Scholastic Teaching Resources

Passage 6: Awesome Travel Experience

1. D; Sample answer: The writer says that Niagara Falls is one of North American's finest natural wonders and that it's awesome. So I know the experience has to be one that's exciting and unusual.

2. C; Sample answer: The other choices are opinions; it is not an opinion that there are fireworks on Friday and Saturday nights.

3. Sample answer: They are headings that help organize ideas so that readers can more easily see what there is to do at Niagara Falls.

4. Sample answer: Ads want you to believe that the place described is so exciting that you will want to go there.

Passage 7: Which Equine?

1. C; Sample answer: The writer says that equines are mammals, which are warm-blooded.

2. B; In paragraph 3, it says that the key contrast is in their heights.

3. Sample answer: Both are small as babies, but only the horse will grow to be taller than 58 inches at the shoulder. Even grown ponies will always have shorter legs, necks, and heads than horses have.

4. Sample answer: The manes and coats of horses are not as thick as they are on ponies, so they can't keep as warm as ponies can.

---

7 Compare & Contrast   Name _____   Date _____

Which Equine?

Read the nature article.
Then follow the directions in the Text Marking box.

Ponies are not baby horses, though people often think they are. In fact, horses and ponies are different animals in the same family. Both are equines (E-kwīnz). Let's compare them.

All equines are mammals. Horses and ponies are warm-blooded. They have backbones and skin covered with hair. Their babies are born live and nurse on the mother's milk. Both horses and ponies can be used for riding, doing farm work, or pulling wagons. Both graze to eat a plant-based diet. They enjoy hay, grass, leaves, fruits, vegetables, and oats.

But these two equines differ in several ways. The key contrast is in their heights. An equine is a horse if it's 58 or more inches tall at the shoulder. Ponies rarely get that tall. They have shorter legs, necks, and heads, and wider bodies than horses do. Ponies cope with cold weather better than horses do because they have thicker manes and coats.

Horses and ponies do not behave the same either. Both can be smart and stubborn, but ponies usually stay calmer than horses do.

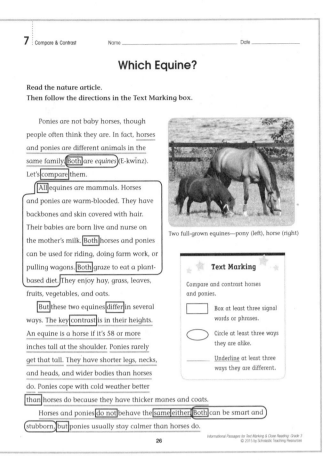
Two full-grown equines—pony (left), horse (right)

★ Text Marking ★

Compare and contrast horses and ponies.

☐ Box at least three signal words or phrases.

◯ Circle at least three ways they are alike.

__ Underline at least three ways they are different.

26

Passage 8: Shopping for Skates

1. A; Sample answer: In paragraph 2, the writer described the leather that figure skates are made of as sturdy and long-lasting.

2. B; According to the article, it is the only statement that describes both figure skates and hockey skates.

3. Sample answer: The special design of each type of skate (boot and blade) helps skaters in ways that fit their sport. Hockey skates make it easier to go fast and change direction quickly. Figure skates help skaters to glide and jump.

4. Sample answers: The hockey skates have a tall part at the top front and back of the boots, probably for extra protection. Also, the blades seem to be attached in different ways.

---

8 Compare & Contrast   Name _____   Date _____

Shopping for Skates

Read the sports article.
Then follow the directions in the Text Marking box.

Anyone can learn to ice skate. All you need is a safe, smooth, icy surface and skates. But which kind of skates should you pick? There are two main choices: hockey skates or figure skates. They differ in their boots and blades.

Boots All ice skates have steel blades attached to the bottoms of boots. Both types of boots lace up the front. Figure-skating boots are made of sturdy, long-lasting leather with thin linings. They give ankle support to skaters for jumps and turns. By contrast, hockey boots are now made of hard plastic with padded linings for protection and comfort.

Blades The blades differ, too. Hockey blades are shorter and narrower than figure-skate blades. This helps hockey players skate fast and quickly change direction. Figure-skating blades are longer and heavier for smooth gliding on ice. Only figure-skate blades have a "toe pick" at the front. This jagged section helps skaters dig into the ice to jump.

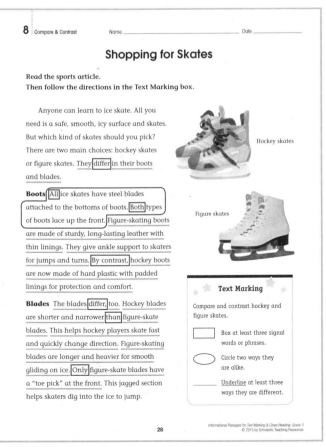
Hockey skates

Figure skates

★ Text Marking ★

Compare and contrast hockey and figure skates.

☐ Box at least three signal words or phrases.

◯ Circle two ways they are alike.

__ Underline at least three ways they are different.

28

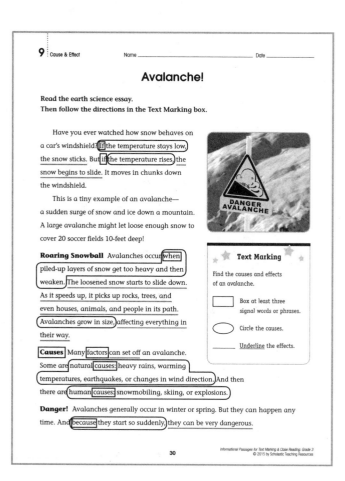

Passage 9: Avalanche!

1. C; Sample answer: The dark-print heading of that paragraph is the clue to what *factors* are.

2. A; Sample answer: It's the only choice not mentioned in the essay.

3. Sample answer: They can happen so suddenly and cause a lot of damage.

4. Sample answer: The author wanted to give an example that readers may know about. Also, it's a simple way to introduce a hard idea.

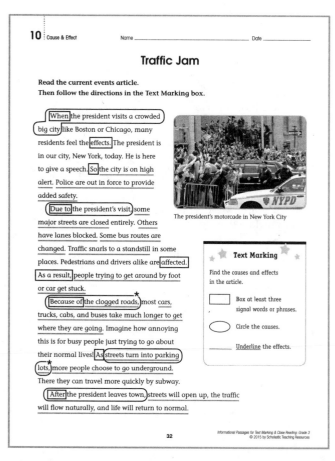

Passage 10: Traffic Jam

1. D; Sample answer: That paragraph talks about pedestrians and drivers, and I found a clue in the last sentence: "people trying to get around by foot or car."

2. A; Sample answer: That is a cause of traffic jams, not an effect.

3. Sample answer: The author means that since the cars aren't moving as they usually do, streets look more like parking lots than active roads with moving cars, buses, and trucks.

4. Sample answer: When the president visits a city, traffic gets really bad, people have a hard time getting around in their usual ways, and some people take the subway if possible.

* The phrases in the passage that are circled and underlined are both causes and effects.

Name That Landform

Read the geography essay.
Then follow the directions in the Text Marking box.

The landscape changes as you drive across America from east to west. In the middle of the country, you see (prairie)—rolling or level grassland with few trees. Prairie land is good for farming and ranching.

As you drive farther west, the land rises. You see many interesting shapes called landforms. These shapes are made of rock and dirt. Each landform has its own name, based on its shape and features.

A (plateau) (pla-TOE) is one kind of landform. It is vast in area and higher than the land around it. A plateau is mostly level, with at least one steep side. Plateaus exist all over the world.

(Mesa) (MAY-sa) is the Spanish word for "table." A mesa is a high landform, smaller than a plateau, with a flat top and steep sides. A (butte) (byoot) is a lone hill or mountain. It is smaller than a mesa. A butte has steep sides and either a flat or rounded top. The top of a butte is much smaller than the top of a mesa.

★ Text Marking ★

Use context clues to unlock word meanings.

⬭ Circle the words *prairie, plateau, mesa,* and *butte* (the first time you read them).

___ Underline context clues for each word.

34

Informational Passages for Text Marking & Close Reading: Grade 3
© 2015 by Scholastic Teaching Resources

◀ Sample Text Markings

Passage 11: Name That Landform

1. C; Sample answer: I figured out that *vast* means very big, which is the same as *huge*.

2. A; Sample answer: A tree is not a shape made of rock and dirt.

3. Sample answer: The prairie would be the best choice because it has few trees and is fairly level grassland, which would be good for growing crops.

4. Sample answer: The bottom photo is the butte because there is much less room at the top than there is in the other landform. The top photo is the mesa. It looks flat like a table.

Fascinating Frogs

Read the life science article.
Then follow the directions in the Text Marking box.

In the fairy tale *The Frog Prince*, an ugly frog kisses a princess and then turns into a handsome prince. They marry and live happily ever after. In real life, frogs don't kiss princesses, but they are otherwise remarkable animals.

Frogs are (amphibians.) All amphibians are cold-blooded—their bodies have the same temperature as the air or water they live in. Amphibians have backbones, no scales, and moist skin. Frogs begin their lives in calm water as eggs and then as tadpoles.

But that just defines frogs. What is interesting is that there are more than 6,300 species of frog! Some are as small as flies, while others are big enough to eat small snakes, mice, and other frogs. Some frogs can jump 10 feet. Some live more than 20 years.

Also interesting is how long frogs have been around. (Herpetologists) (HUR-puh-tol-oh-jists)—the scientists who study amphibians and snakes—know that frogs have existed for at least 200 million years! They were here along with the dinosaurs.

European tree frog

★ Text Marking ★

Use context clues to unlock word meanings.

⬭ Circle the words *amphibians* and *herpetologists* (the first time you read them).

___ Underline context clues for each word.

36

Informational Passages for Text Marking & Close Reading: Grade 3
© 2015 by Scholastic Teaching Resources

◀ Sample Text Markings

Passage 12: Fascinating Frogs

1. B; Sample answer: Since frogs start their lives in water, *moist* must mean wet, or damp.

2. A; Sample answer: According to the article, all the other choices about frogs are true. Plus, it says that amphibians have no scales.

3. Sample answer: In paragraph 2, it says that frogs are amphibians, and all amphibians are cold-blooded.

4. Sample answer: The author did this to get the reader's attention and to bring up the idea that real frogs are fascinating even though they do not turn into princes.

Musical Memory

Read the music article.
Then follow the directions in the Text Marking box.

Musicians enjoy performing. Learning to play correctly takes time and effort. To perform well, musicians must learn every note, when to play loudly or softly, quickly or slowly, and when to pause. But that is not enough.

The best musicians believe that performing from memory gets the best results. Memorizing music sounds very hard. But there is a proven answer: practice, practice, practice!

Before trying to memorize any piece, learn to play it as written. Follow any method your music teacher suggests. Practice until you can play the whole piece perfectly.

Now focus on memorizing. This takes time, but it works. Start small. Focus on short sections, such as a line or two of music. Repeat three times without error. Continue until you can do this without looking at the music. Muscles remember what you practice.

Next, memorize longer chunks, such as a full page. Repeat without error again and again to train your brain and muscles to know just what to do. The problem of memorizing a piece disappears. You're ready to perform!

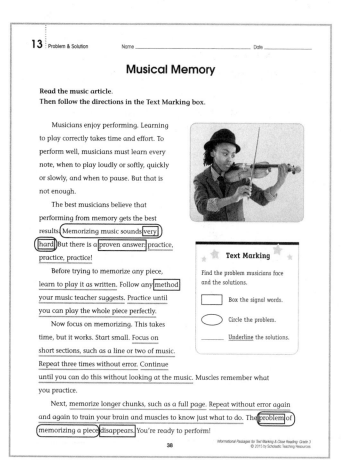

> **Text Marking**
>
> Find the problem musicians face and the solutions.
>
> ▢ Box the signal words.
>
> ◯ Circle the problem.
>
> ___ Underline the solutions.

38

◀ Sample Text Markings

Passage 13: Musical Memory

1. C; Sample answer: The main idea of the article is how to play a piece by heart so you can perform it well.

2. D; Sample answer: The article says that you must learn the piece first as it is written before trying to play it from memory.

3. Sample answer: According to this article, when you play a piece over and over, your brain and muscles learn what to do and when.

4. Sample answer: First learn the piece perfectly with the written music. Then, practice small parts until you don't need to look at the music. Repeat until you know the whole piece by heart.

Work Wear

Read the historical anecdote.
Then follow the directions in the Text Marking box.

In 1849, gold was discovered in California. Men from far and wide flocked there to seek their fortunes. Business people followed the "forty-niners" to sell them clothing, supplies, and mining gear. Levi Strauss was one of these people. He arrived in California in 1853 to sell fabric and other goods.

In those days, work was as hard on clothing as it was on people. It was a problem for workers to get sturdy clothing that would last.

A solution arose in 1872, when Strauss got a letter from Jacob Davis. Davis was a tailor who had bought fabric from him. He used *rivets* instead of just thread to hold pants together in a better way. Davis thought rivets could make pants last longer, but he wanted Strauss's help. The men became partners.

On May 20, 1873, Levi Strauss and Jacob Davis got a *patent*. This legal paper gave them the right to make and sell riveted work pants. And so they did. Their "waist overalls"—the very first blue jeans—were a hit. Rivets made all the difference.

An old Levi Strauss advertisement

> **Text Marking**
>
> Find the problem workers faced.
> Find the solution.
>
> ▢ Box the signal words.
>
> ◯ Circle the problem.
>
> ___ Underline the solution.

> **rivet:** short metal fastener more long-lasting than thread

40

◀ Sample Text Markings

Passage 14: Work Wear

1. B; Sample answer: In that paragraph, it said that the men came from far and wide and were eager to find gold, so I figured it means that many of them went.

2. C; Sample answer: The sturdy work pants with rivets were the product Strauss and his partner presented to the world.

3. Sample answer: The ad shows horses pulling the pants in two directions. You would expect them to rip apart, but the ad says, "It's no use, can't be ripped." This ad brags about how sturdy and rugged the pants were.

4. Sample answer: Davis had the idea about using rivets to make better pants. Strauss already had a business selling things to workers. Together, they changed how work pants were made and made them popular.

Name _____ Date _____

L-o-n-g Sandwiches

Read the word origin article.
Then follow the directions in the Text Marking box.

Have you seen those (oversized) (sandwiches) that are popular at parties? Picture (a long roll stuffed with meat, cheese, and veggies.) Some gigantic versions can be 10-feet long. Those monsters are carried on a board so they hold their shape.

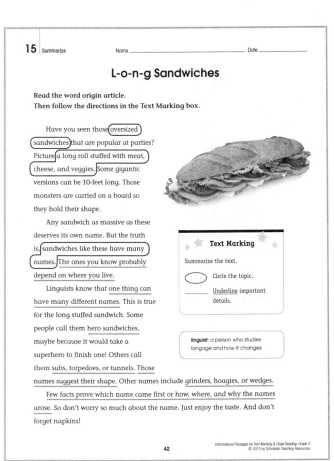

Any sandwich as massive as these deserves its own name. But the truth is, (sandwiches like these have many names.) The ones you know probably depend on where you live.

Linguists know that one thing can have many different names. This is true for the long stuffed sandwich. Some people call them hero sandwiches, maybe because it would take a superhero to finish one! Others call them subs, torpedoes, or tunnels. Those names suggest their shape. Other names include grinders, hoagies, or wedges.

Few facts prove which name came first or how, where, and why the names arose. So don't worry so much about the name. Just enjoy the taste. And don't forget napkins!

> ★ **Text Marking** ★
>
> Summarize the text.
>
> ◯ Circle the topic.
>
> __ Underline important details.

> **linguist:** a person who studies langage and how it changes

42

Informational Passages for Text Marking & Close Reading: Grade 3
© 2015 by Scholastic Teaching Resources

◀ Sample Text Markings

Passage 15: L-o-n-g Sandwiches

1. B; Sample answer: The article is about huge sandwiches, and *massive* is another word for *enormous*.

2. A; Sample answer: The author talks about all the different names this kind of sandwich can have, so this title gets at the main idea of the article.

3. Sample answer: This article talks about the many names the long, stuffed sandwich can have, depending on where you live. The author includes seven different names but admits that there are few facts to prove where, why, when, or how these names came about.

4. Sample answer: Monsters are usually big and scary. I think the author is poking fun at those huge sandwiches, which some people might find scary to eat because they are so big and messy.

Name _____ Date _____

Puppets That Dance on Water

Read the cultural arts essay.
Then follow the directions in the Text Marking box.

A puppet is a kind of doll moved by hand. Somebody who performs this work is called a puppeteer. Puppets can be made from all kinds of materials and are often used to amuse or teach.

(Puppetry is an art form in many cultures.) Vietnam is a long, narrow country in southeast Asia, near China. Vietnam borders the sea. Its long tradition of puppetry goes back almost 1,000 years. (One form is called *mua roi nuroc*, which means "puppets that dance on water.") This is exactly what they appear to do.

Water puppets on a dragon boat

Water puppets are carved of wood and then painted. Each puppet is supported by a long rod hidden under the water. Puppeteers pull strings and wires to make the parts of a puppet move. The stage is a pool of water several feet deep. The puppeteers stand in the water behind a screen to work the puppets.

Water puppet shows are usually held at outdoor festivals. Musicians play as the puppets act out folktales, myths, or stories about village life.

> ★ **Text Marking** ★
>
> Summarize the text.
>
> ◯ Circle the topic.
>
> __ Underline important details.

44

Informational Passages for Text Marking & Close Reading: Grade 3
© 2015 by Scholastic Teaching Resources

◀ Sample Text Markings

Passage 16: Puppets That Dance on Water

1. B; Sample answer: The essay says puppets are like dolls which kids play with to have fun. Plus, I picture water puppet shows as fun and entertaining.

2. C; Sample answer: Paragraph 3 starts by saying, "Water puppets are carved of wood."

3. Sample answer: Vietnam has a long tradition of puppetry, especially with its colorful water puppets. Puppeteers work them in water, with music playing. The puppets are used to act out stories.

4. Sample answer: It looks like it might be a folktale or myth because people in fancy costumes or clothes are riding a dragon. The people are traveling somewhere— maybe for an adventure, a festival, or a rescue.

Informational Passages for Text Marking & Close Reading: Grade 3
© 2015 by Scholastic Teaching Resources

"Why Not?"

Read the biographical sketch.
Then follow the directions in the Text Marking box.

Lonnie Johnson always loved taking things apart. Sometimes he put them back together. Other times, he combined odd parts to make new things. He learned how to use tools from his dad.

At 13, Lonnie put an old engine on a homemade go-cart. He loved zooming around in it. He dreamed of being an inventor.

By high school, Lonnie built a remote-control robot from junk. This won him first prize at the Alabama State Science Fair. His friends called him "The Professor." In college, Lonnie was an honor student. Later, he became an Air Force officer, rocket scientist, and business leader. But he never stopped inventing.

Dr. Lonnie Johnson in his lab

> ★ **Text Marking** ★
>
> Make an inference: What helped Dr. Lonnie Johnson reach his dream?
>
> _____ Underline text clues.
>
> 💡 Think about what you already know.

You may have played with his most famous invention—the Super Soaker®. Lonnie got the idea for this power-squirt toy while working on another invention. When he tested a homemade part in his bathroom, it shot water across the room.

Today, Dr. Lonnie Johnson has more than 100 successful inventions. He remains curious and keeps trying new things.

46

Informational Passages for Text Marking & Close Reading: Grade 3
© 2015 by Scholastic Teaching Resources

◀ Sample Text Markings

Passage 17: "Why Not?"

1. C; Sample answer: In paragraph 3, it says that Lonnie won first prize at the Alabama State Science Fair, which impressed his friends. They realized how very smart he was.

2. A; Sample answer: In paragraph 4, it says that he didn't start out with the idea for the Super Soaker. He got the idea when he was working on a different invention. So it was by accident.

3. Sample answer: I think it shows that Dr. Johnson didn't take no for an answer. He wanted to try his ideas himself to see if they would work or not.

4. Sample answer: I think Dr. Johnson reached his dream because he never stopped inventing. He spent his life inventing things and is still at it. I think he worked hard in his life and never took no for an answer.

Food for Thought

Read the nutrition article.
Then follow the directions in the Text Marking box.

Does it matter how much fat, salt, and sugar children eat? Should kids avoid fatty foods like chicken fingers and French fries? Should they steer clear of salty junk foods, like puffed cheese sticks? Should they stay away from foods loaded with chemicals and dyes? Soda has both.

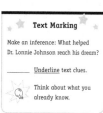

Fat, salt, and sugar make foods taste good. But too much of a good thing can harm you. That's why food scientists strongly support healthy eating. They want to direct children and parents toward wiser food choices. Teachers, school nurses, doctors, and many parents agree. They hope schools will share the responsibility of keeping kids fit and strong.

A healthy salad

> ★ **Text Marking** ★
>
> Make an inference: What worries the author of this article?
>
> _____ Underline text clues.
>
> 💡 Think about what you already know.

So, many school communities urge cafeteria lunches to be both tasty *and* nourishing. They encourage serving wholesome, natural foods. They don't want kids eating foods with unhealthy ingredients in them. And scientists and educators want school lunches to be varied. They suggest that menus celebrate cultural differences.

Teachers and principals care deeply about how kids learn best. Science shows that a healthy diet increases a child's ability to stay alert for learning. That is surely food for thought.

48

Informational Passages for Text Marking & Close Reading: Grade 3
© 2015 by Scholastic Teaching Resources

◀ Sample Text Markings

Passage 18: Food for Thought

1. A; Sample answer: Junk foods are mentioned in the first paragraph, which describes foods to avoid.

2. C; Sample answer: In the first paragraph, the words *avoid, steer clear,* and *stay away from* seem to mean the same thing.

3. Sample answer: The writer worries that kids eat too much junk food—food that has too much salt, sugar, fat, and chemicals, and not enough healthy nutritious food.

4. Sample answer: According to the article, science shows that a healthy diet helps children learn better. Also, teachers believe that schools can share the responsibility for keeping kids alert, fit, and strong.

Informational Passages for Text Marking & Close Reading: Grade 3
© 2015 by Scholastic Teaching Resources

19 Author's Purpose   Name _____ Date _____

As Fit as a Clown

Read the physical education article.
Then follow the directions in the Text Marking box.

(I) Are you "circus fit"? Big-top performers are. They need to be in peak condition. How else could they perform all those wacky stunts? How do they juggle while balancing on a rope? How do they ride around backwards on a unicycle?

To do all this nutty stuff, circus performers exercise a lot. They must be as strong as they are silly. They must be as fit (I) as they are funny. One major circus now shares its fitness secrets with kids. Clowns, dancers, and acrobats visit schools to teach what they do to stay in shape.

Kids who take part may not learn to prance about in huge flapping shoes. (I) But they will learn how to be strong and flexible. They will get tips for keeping fit and staying safe. Plus, they may learn riddles like this one:

   Q: Why do lions like to eat high-wire artists?
(E)   **A:** Because they want a well-balanced meal!

(I) When that circus comes to town, the kids get to attend. Some lucky ones may even step into the ring and perform!

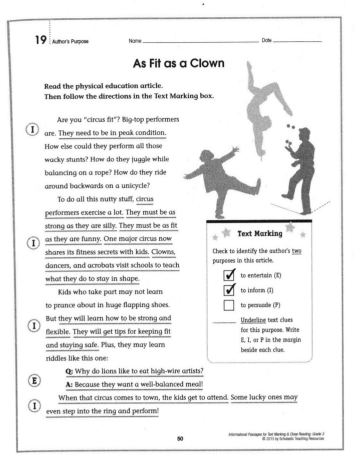

Text Marking

Check to identify the author's **two** purposes in this article.

- [✓] to entertain (E)
- [✓] to inform (I)
- [ ] to persuade (P)

_____ Underline text clues for this purpose. Write E, I, or P in the margin beside each clue.

50

Informational Passages for Text Marking & Close Reading: Grade 3
© 2015 by Scholastic Teaching Resources

◀ Sample Text Markings

Passage 19: As Fit as a Clown

1. D; Sample answer: *Peak condition* means the most fit you can be, and a pro athlete would need to be that fit.

2. C; Sample answer: The article said nothing about those other skills, only that clowns teach kids how to be fit.

3. Sample answer: The riddle is funny because it is a play on words—balancing well on a high wire is different than a well-balanced meal. The author included it to entertain readers.

4. Sample answer: The author does two things. One is to inform readers that circus performers are not just funny—they are strong and in great physical shape. The other is to entertain with a joke and by describing some funny things you see at a circus.

---

20 Author's Purpose   Name _____ Date _____

A Pool in Every School

Read the letter to the editor.
Then follow the directions in the Text Marking box.

To the Editor:

We citizens expect our schools to be well equipped. We make sure that our children have classrooms supplied with the latest technology and the most effective educational equipment. We also favor having organized and well-outfitted athletics programs, from soccer to gymnastics. But shouldn't our schools provide (P) one more kind of training for our students: a swimming program?

Every child should learn how to swim. (P) Swimming improves fitness and health. Swimmers develop strong muscles. Plus, swimming is a lifetime pleasure. It's so enjoyable to leap from a dock into a still lake or glide down a winding water slide into a welcoming pool. And snorkeling or diving underwater to see colorful fish and beautiful coral is a blast!

But there is a more important reason why all kids should become good (P) swimmers: safety in water. For that key reason alone, our schools should teach students to swim.

So I urge all schools to offer swimming instruction—for fun, for fitness, (P) and for safety. Let's put a pool in every school!

Nora Liu

El Paso, TX

Text Marking

Check to identify the author's purpose in this letter.

- [ ] to entertain (E)
- [ ] to inform (I)
- [✓] to persuade (P)

_____ Underline text clues for this purpose. Write E, I, or P in the margin beside each clue.

52

Informational Passages for Text Marking & Close Reading: Grade 3
© 2015 by Scholastic Teaching Resources

◀ Sample Text Markings

Passage 20: A Pool in Every School

1. D; Sample answer: The first paragraph talks about well-equipped schools and about classrooms having all the things needed by teachers and students to make learning happen best.

2. A; Sample answer: It is the only choice not discussed in the letter.

3. Sample answer: Her idea may not be practical because some schools have no room to add pools. Also, they cost a lot of money to build.

4. Sample answer: The author is writing this piece to convince others that having a school swimming program is an excellent idea for all schools and all children.

Informational Passages for Text Marking & Close Reading: Grade 3
© 2015 by Scholastic Teaching Resources

Notes